CHRISTMAS DECORATING

CHRISTMAS DECORATING

HOW TO MAKE AND DECORATE
YOUR OWN FESTIVE BAUBLES,
WREATHS, CANDLES, STOCKINGS,
CRACKERS AND TREE DECORATIONS

EDITED BY CAROLYN BELL

southwater

This edition published by Southwater

Distributed in the UK by
The Manning Partnership
251–253 London Road East
Batheaston
Bath BA1 7RL
tel. 01225 852 727
fax 01225 852 852

Published in the USA by
Anness Publishing Inc.
27 West 20th Street
Suite 504
New York
NY 10011
fax 212 807 6813

Distributed in Canada by
General Publishing
895 Don Mills Road
400–402 Park Centre
Toronto, Ontario M3C 1W3
tel. 416 445 3333
fax 416 445 5991

Distributed in Australia by
Sandstone Publishing
Unit 1, 360 Norton Street
Leichhardt
New South Wales 2040
tel. 02 9560 7888
fax 02 9560 7488

Southwater is an imprint of Anness Publishing Limited
Hermes House, 88–89 Blackfriars Road, London SE1 8HA
tel. 020 7401 2077; fax 020 7633 9499

© Anness Publishing Limited 2001

Publisher: Joanna Lorenz
Senior Managing Editor: Judith Simons
Senior Editor: Doreen Palamartschuk
Indexer: Hilary Bird
Photography: Steve Dalton, James Duncan, Michelle Garrett, Nelson Hargreaves,
Don Last, Debbie Patterson, Anthony Pickhaver, Peter Williams, Mark Wood, Polly Wreford
Craft Projects: Michael Ball, Fiona Barnett, Petra Boase, Penny Boylan, Marion Elliot, Tessa Evelegh,
Emma Hardy, Christine Kingdom, Mary Maguire, Terence Moore, Isabel Stanley,
Sally Walton, Pamela Westland
Designers: Jane Coney, Ian Sandom
Editorial Reader: Joy Wotton
Production Controller: Claire Rae

Also published as part of a larger compendium, *The Complete Book of Christmas*

1 3 5 7 9 10 8 6 4 2

For all craft projects, quantities are given in both metric and imperial measurements, and, where appropriate,
measures are also given in standard cups and spoons. Follow one set, but not a mixture,
because they are not interchangeable. Bracketed terms are intended for American readers.

CONTENTS

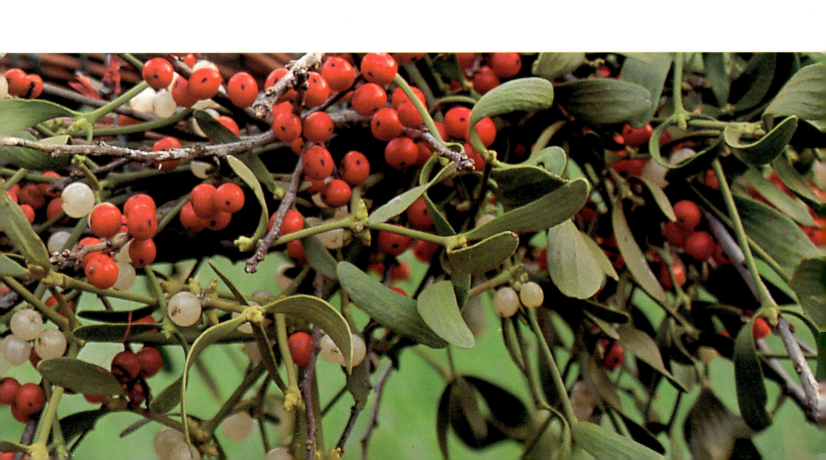

INTRODUCTION

There's no time like Christmas. Sooner or later we all get swept up in its huge, warm embrace. It may be commercialized, expensive and a lot of hard work, but it can also be a magical time of happy gatherings and memorable meals, reaffirming friendships and family ties.

Christmas is an unrivalled opportunity to give free rein to your creativity as you decorate your home and plan your festive table. Brighten the dark days of winter with the glint of gold, the enchanting glow of candlelight and the scent of freshly gathered evergreens. These lovely craft ideas will spark your creative energy and help you make the best of the season.

You'll find suggestions for traditional tree ornaments, or you may prefer an elegant, modern arrangement of gold or silver. If you'd rather get

ABOVE: *Use painted clothes pegs to hang your cards up the stairs.*

LEFT: *Turn plain glass Christmas tree ornaments into opulent gilded decorations by covering them in swirling patterns of gold glass (relief) outliner.*

right away from Christmas glitz, find inspiration in a rustic look, using materials such as homespun fabrics, raffia, and twigs and greenery you could collect on a winter walk.

Don't stop at making decorations: create your own gift-wrap and tags – and gifts too. Find out how to make your own crackers and you'll be able to fill them with personalized treats for your guests.

All the projects are simple to make following the detailed step-by-step instructions. Perhaps they'll introduce you to some new skills, such as flower arranging or stencilling, that you'll want to develop after the flurry of Christmas is over. Once you've discovered the satisfaction that comes from creating your own Christmas you'll no longer be content with ready-made decorations. Collect rich fabrics, gold paper, ribbons, glitter and paint and use them to turn your home into a welcoming haven every Christmas.

RIGHT: *Natural materials make lovely decorations: collect your own evergreens, nuts and cones.*

7

Materials and Equipment

*W*hen you make your own Christmas decorations you can use good-quality, lavish materials. However, you do not have to spend vast amounts as you will only need to use small amounts of beautiful fabrics, ribbons and braids to create an illusion of opulence. Throughout the year, collect interesting materials for your projects: save pretty boxes, old cards and gift-wrap, foil wrapping and attractive packaging material. To save time, ensure you have all necessary materials before you begin a project, many are household items that are not difficult to acquire.

PAPERS AND PAINTS

Build up a store of interesting materials for your decorating projects:

save pretty boxes, foil wrapping and packaging material.

CRAYONS AND PENS

Stencil crayons come in a range of plain and metallic colours. They are oil-based and dry out to form a skin which must be scraped away each time they are used. Allow the work to dry thoroughly for a permanent finish. Gold (magic) marker pens are an alternative to paint when you need a fine line.

DECORATIVE PAPERS

The choice is endless here. Look for double-sided and metallic crêpe paper, especially in unusual colours such as bronze. Gold papers and foils come in various textures, matt and shiny, and add a touch of luxury to your work. Don't forget the basics: add your own decorations to brown parcel wrap (packaging paper), white paper and card (cardboard).

GLITTER AND GLITTER PAINTS

There is an amazing selection of different types of glitter to choose from now. As well as the old-fashioned tubes of coloured glitter to sprinkle on, you can buy coloured glitter suspended in clear paint and tubes of glittery fabric paints.

LINO-CUTTING TOOL

This can be used to cut decorative grooves in citrus fruit. Another traditional implement, used by chefs, is a canelle knife.

METAL FOILS

Copper and aluminium foils are available from crafts suppliers in a heavier gauge than ordinary kitchen foil.

OIL-BASED PAINTS

These are used for decorating surfaces that will need washing, such as glass and ceramics. Read the manufacturer's instructions before you use them. Clean your brushes with (distilled) turpentine or white spirit (paint thinner). Glass (relief) outliner paint comes in a tube and is squeezed directly on to the surface. It needs a long drying time but sets hard.

OTHER PAINTS

Gold spray paint is useful for covering large areas, but look out for different shades of gold in water-based and oil-based paints. Watercolour inks have a wonderful translucent vibrancy that is quite different to the matt effect of gouache paint.

PAPERS

There is a tremendous range of decorative papers available from stationers and craft suppliers. It is always worth stocking up at Christmas time.

POLYSTYRENE SHAPES (PLASTIC FOAM FORMS)

These are available from craft suppliers and come in a large range of different shapes.

WHITE EMULSION (LATEX) PAINT

This is a cheaper alternative to white gouache paint for covering the surface of papier-mâché. For added strength, mix in some PVA (white) glue.

WILLOW TWIGS

Perfect for rustic decorations, willow twigs grow straight and are very pliable.

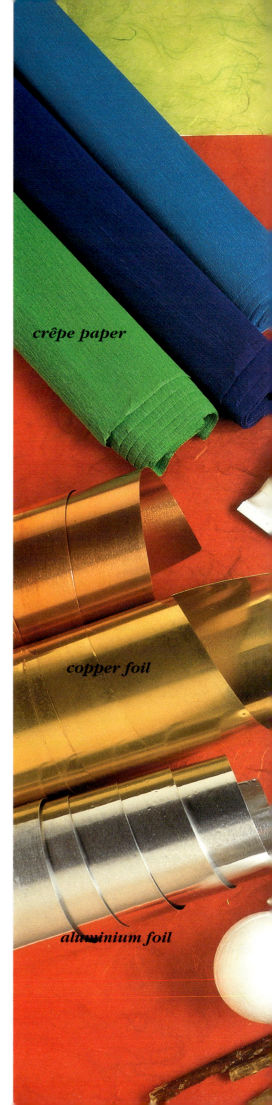

crêpe paper

copper foil

aluminium foil

metallic
crêpe paper

gold spray paint

card
(cardboard)

stencil crayons

gold relief
outliner

white
paper

white emulsion
(latex) paint

oil-based
glass paint

gouache

foam
board

lino-cutting tool

decorative
papers

gold water-
based paint

watercolour inks

glitter paint

glitter

polystyrene shapes
(plastic foam forms)

gold (magic)
marker pen

willow twigs

foil wrappers

FABRICS AND THREADS

One of the joys of making your own decorations lies in using high-quality, sumptuous materials. You can create an impression of luxury with very small amounts of beautiful fabrics, ribbons and braids.

BUTTONS
Many people collect buttons for pleasure. For Christmas, keep a supply of gold buttons and always save real mother-of-pearl buttons from shirts that are no longer used.

CHECKED COTTON, TICKING, WOOL, CALICO, HESSIAN (BURLAP) AND LINEN
As an antidote to all the richness of traditional Christmas fabrics, simple, country-style, homespun materials are perfect for naïve decorations. Age fabrics by washing them well, then dipping in strong tea.

CORDS AND BRAIDS
Gold is the most festive colour for cords and braids. Use fine gold cord to make loops for hanging decorations on the tree.

POLYESTER WADDING (BATTING)
This is invaluable for stuffing since it is lightweight and very soft. It can also be purchased in lengths for quilting, which can be cut to shape when a light padding is needed.

RIBBONS
Wide satin ribbon is the kind most often used for the projects in this book. Wire-edged ribbon is very good for making bows.

SEQUINS AND BEADS
Seed pearls (heads), sequins and glass beads add instant opulence to any decorative piece. They are available from crafts suppliers in a multitude of shapes.

SILKS, TAFFETA, ORGANZA (ORGANDY) AND LAMÉ
Use these luxurious fabrics for decorations and gifts. You'll find plenty of gold shades to choose from in the run-up to Christmas.

STRING AND RAFFIA
Thin garden twine is used for several of the projects in this book: its soft brown colour and rustic appearance suit naïve decorations. Sisal (parcel string) and natural (garden) raffia are also used.

TAPESTRY CANVAS
You will need white canvas with 24 holes to 5cm (12 holes to 1in) for any needlepoint projects in this book.

THREADS
A well-stocked sewing box filled with every shade of sewing thread is every dressmaker's dream. Start with essential black and white and build up your collection as you sew. Stranded embroidery thread (floss) has six strands: for all but the boldest stitches you'll probably want to use two or three. Tapestry wool (yarn) is for canvas work and is very hardwearing. Don't be tempted to substitute knitting wool (yarn) or you will get constant breaks as you stitch.

VELVET
Available in rich, dark colours, velvet is especially Christmassy. It is available in light weights for dressmaking and heavier weights for furnishing (upholstering).

homespun cotton check

calico

linen

polyester wadding (batting)

tapestry canvas

hessian (burlap)

pleated organza

lamé

velvet

cotton ticking

gold netting

fine gold cord

decorative braid

gold braid

silk

sequin ribbon

glass beads

plastic gemstones

mother-of-pearl buttons

sewing thread

satin ribbons

garden twine

stranded embroidery thread (floss)

quilting wadding (batting)

sisal (parcel string)

tapestry wool (yarn)

natural (garden) raffia

EQUIPMENT

It's sensible to make sure you have everything you need for your Christmas craft project

before you begin. The following list includes artist's materials, office supplies and some

basic equipment you probably already have around the home.

ADHESIVE TAPE
Double-sided adhesive tape allows you to join paper invisibly. It is also a substitute for glue when you don't wish to dampen a surface such as crêpe paper.

CRAFT KNIFE
These have extremely sharp blades. Use them for cutting out stencils and for accurate cutting of paper against a metal ruler. Change the blade frequently and keep out of the reach of children. Always use with a cutting mat.

CUTTING MAT
Use when cutting out with a craft knife to protect your work surface. A self-healing mat is best.

FOAM ROLLERS
These come in assorted sizes and are easily washable. Use them with stencil paint and for sponging water-based paints on to paper or fabrics.

GLUE
PVA (white) glue is a thick liquid that dries to a transparent sheen. It can be diluted with water when making papier-mâché or as a protective coating. After use, wash brushes in water straight away. Glue sticks are excellent for sticking paper and are safe for children to use.

HOLE PUNCH
Useful for making neat holes for the handles of gift bags and for punching holes in gift tags.

HOT GLUE GUN
The nozzle delivers a small dot of hot, melted glue. The glue dries almost instantly.

METAL RULER
This provides a safe edge to work against when cutting paper with a craft knife.

PAINTBRUSHES
Old brushes are useful for applying glue and emulsion (latex) paint mixed with PVA (white) glue. Stencil brushes are wide and stiff. You will need a fine-tipped brush for delicate work and a medium bristle brush for applying metallic craft paint, which should be cleaned with white spirit (paint thinner).

PENCILS, PENS AND MARKERS
A soft pencil that can easily be erased is useful for tracing motifs. Keep an old ballpoint pen that has run out of ink for making embossed foil decorations. For marking light fabrics, use a vanishing fabric marker.

PINS AND NEEDLES
Use dressmaker's pins to hold fabrics in place. Use an ordinary sewing needle for seams and an embroidery needle for embroidery thread (floss). A tapestry needle is fairly broad, with a large eye and a blunt point.

PLASTIC ADHESIVE
This malleable substance is used for attaching objects and paper to surfaces from which it can later be removed cleanly.

SCISSORS
You will need one pair for cutting paper and another for fabrics: never use the latter on paper as it will blunt them very quickly. A small pair of needle-work scissors with pointed ends is useful for embroidery.

SECATEURS (PRUNING SHEARS)
Used to cut heavy-duty foliage and for twig decorations.

STAPLER AND STAPLE GUN
A staple gun is indispensable for attaching fabrics to wood or board. An ordinary office stapler will secure paper, fabric and thin card (cardboard).

STENCIL CARD (CARDBOARD)
Specially made for stencilling, this is coated in a water-resistant oil so that you can wipe it clean between stencils, and when changing colours. Transfer your image to the card using a soft pencil and cut it out with a craft knife.

TAPE MEASURE
A tape measure is more flexible than a ruler, and is therefore suitable for measuring lengths of fabric.

TRACING PAPER
Trace a motif and cut it out to use as a pattern. Alternatively, transfer it by rubbing the back of the tracing paper with a soft pencil, positioning the template, and then tracing over the outline again from the front of the paper.

cutting mat

double-sided
adhesive tape

PVA (white)
glue

staple gun

foam roller

craft knife

metal ruler

hole punch

needles

tracing
paper

pins

tape
measure

scissors

stapler

stencil
brush

fine-tipped
brush

fabric
marker

hot glue
gun

encil card
rdboard)

plastic adhesive

ballpoint
pen

pencil

permanent
marker

secateurs
(pruning
shears)

Wreaths and Table Decorations

*B*ringing evergreens indoors to decorate the house is very traditional. There are many ideas here for making a welcoming wreath for the front door, a garland for indoors and a gorgeous swag for the mantelpiece. Candle pots make lovely table centrepieces, and you can even create a miniature Topiary Tree. Many natural materials such as blue pine (spruce), cinnamon sticks and dried rosemary have the spicy smell that is the true essence of Christmas. Experiment with new versions of favourite designs, such as the Mistletoe Kissing Ring, or for real impact make a stunning Tulip and Holly Wreath.

Traditional Christmas Wreath

Blue pine (spruce) releases a glorious fresh scent as you work with it. Here it is used with

dried red roses and amaranthus for a traditional look.

MATERIALS

large copper or steel garland ring
sphagnum moss
silver reel (rose) wire
secateurs (pruning shears)
blue pine (spruce)
dried amaranthus, dyed red
medium stub wires
dried red roses
dried lavender
natural (garden) raffia
twigs
sweet chestnuts
fir cones
dried fungi
strong florist's wire

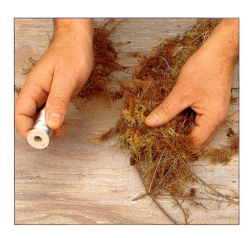

1 Cover the ring very roughly on both sides with moss – this need not be thick but should be fairly even. Secure the moss in place by winding with silver reel (rose) wire, leaving a space of about 5cm/2in between each loop.

2 Trim the blue pine (spruce) to lengths of about 15–20cm/6–8in. Divide into four piles and begin to tie each stem to the ring with wire, using one pile for each quarter of the ring. Work outward from the inner edge in a zigzag fashion.

3 Trim the amaranthus stems to 20cm/8in and wire into four small bunches, leaving the stub wires untrimmed. Treat the roses in the same way, but cut the stems to 10cm/4in. In each quarter of the ring, push a bunch or roses and a bunch of amaranthus, tying the wires into the back of the ring.

4 Trim the lavender to 20cm/8in and wire into four bunches. Keep a long length of wire hanging from each bunch and wind a bow of raffia around the stems. Push each wire through the blue pine (spruce) and tie to the back.

5 Wire bunches of twigs, chestnuts, fir cones and fungi. Tie bows of raffia around the bunches of twigs. Add these materials in small mixed groups, linking each group around the ring. Add a loop of strong wire to the back of the garland for hanging and tie a raffia bow at the top.

Kumquat Wreath

Vibrant orange kumquats and green chillies give a traditional wreath a modern twist.

MATERIALS

secateurs (pruning shears)
sprigs of bay leaves
blue pine (spruce)
medium stub wires
kumquats
green chillies
small fir cones
small willow or
vine wreath base
scissors
wide wire-edged ribbon
dressmaker's pin

2 Twist a piece of wire around each stem, leaving a length to insert into the willow wreath base.

5 Reserving a short length of ribbon for the centre of the bow, join the ends together with a pin.

1 Trim the bay leaves and blue pine (spruce) into sprigs suitable for the size of the wreath, wiring pieces together here and there to fill them out.

3 Wire the kumquats and chillies by sticking a piece of wire through the base, then bending the ends down and twisting them together. Wind a piece of wire around the base of each fir cone.

6 Fold the ribbon over on itself to make four loops.

7 Pinch the centre of the loops together and secure with a wire. Cover this with the remaining piece of ribbon and then wire the bow to the top of the wreath.

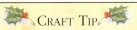
CRAFT TIP

*R*eady-made rings made from natural materials such as willow and vines are available from florists in many different sizes. You could also make your own ring using vines or twigs cut when they are green.

4 Attach the greenery, kumquats, chillies and fir cones to the wreath, twisting the ends of the wires to secure them.

CLEMENTINE WREATH

This colourful wreath is very modern in its regular geometry and its

bold use of tightly grouped materials and vivid colours.

MATERIALS

medium stub wires
clementines
30cm/12in diameter florist's foam ring
secateurs (pruning shears)
pyracanthus branches, with
berries and leaves
ivy leaves

1 Push a stub wire across and through the base of each clementine from one side to the other, and bend the two projecting ends down. Bend another wire to form a hairpin shape and push the ends right through the middle of each clementine so that the bend in the wire is sitting flush with the top of the fruit. Cut the projecting wires to about 4cm/1½in.

2 Soak the plastic foam ring in water. Arrange two rows of wired clementines in tight circles on the ring by pushing their projecting wire legs into the foam.

3 Cut the pyracanthus into stems about 6cm/2½in long. Push the stems into the outer side of the plastic ring and between the two rings of clementines, making sure it is evenly distributed.

4 Cut the ivy leaves into individual stems about 7cm/3in long. Push the stems into the plastic, positioning a leaf between each clementine.

Tulip and Holly Wreath

This gorgeous wreath can be used on a door or, with candles, as a table centrepiece.

MATERIALS

25cm/10in diameter florist's foam ring
100 white tulips
scissors
holly with berries

1 Soak the plastic foam ring in water. Cut the tulips to a stem length of approximately 3cm/1¼in. Starting at the centre, work outward in concentric circles to cover the whole surface of the plastic foam with tulip heads.

2 Cover any exposed foam and the outside of the ring with holly leaves by pushing the stems into the foam and overlapping them flat against the edge of the ring. Make sure you don't leave any gaps in the foam.

3 Cut 12 stems of holly with berries approximately 4cm/1½in long. Push them into the foam in two concentric circles around the ring, one towards the inside and the other towards the outside. Make sure no foam is still visible.

CRAFT TIP

The tulip stems are pushed fully into the foam in tight masses, so that only their heads are visible.

Mistletoe Kissing Ring

A traditional kissing ring can be hung up as a Christmas decoration to serve

as a focal point for a seasonal kiss.

MATERIALS

scissors
7 stems of winterberry, with berries
large bunch of mistletoe
twine
twisted cane ring
tartan (plaid) ribbon

1 Cut the stems of the winterberry into 18cm/7in lengths. Divide the mistletoe into 14 substantial stems and make the smaller sprigs into bunches by tying with twine. Attach some winterberry on to the outside of the cane ring with the twine. Add a stem, or bunch, of mistletoe so that it overlaps about one-third of the length of winterberry, and bind in place. Bind on another stem of winterberry, overlapping the mistletoe.

2 Repeat the sequence until the outside of the ring is covered in a "herringbone" pattern of materials. Cut four lengths of ribbon of approximately 60cm/24in each. Tie one end of each piece of ribbon to the decorated ring at four equidistant points around its circumference. Bring the ends of the ribbon up above the ring and tie in a bow for hanging.

Topiary Tree

Make a small ornamental tree for indoors, or a large tree to place outside the front door.

MATERIALS

terracotta flowerpot
setting clay
small tree trunk or thick branch
florist's foam sphere
strong glue
silver reel (rose) wire
secateurs (pruning shears)
blue pine (spruce)
sphagnum moss
medium stub wires
small dried red roses
fir cones
hand drill and vice or hot glue gun
assorted nuts
cinnamon sticks
dried rosemary stalks
natural (garden) raffia

2 Using stub wires, wire the roses into small bunches, leaving a long length of wire to insert into the foam sphere. Add the roses to the tree at random, pressing the stub wires well into each area of the round foam shape.

5 Tie stub wires around the cinnamon sticks and rosemary stalks to make small bundles, again leaving long lengths of wire. Cover the wire with raffia tied in a bow. Add the bundles to the tree.

1 Cover the inside of the flowerpot with setting clay, then push the trunk into the centre. Add more clay to half-fill the pot. Leave to set hard. Push the foam sphere on to the top of the trunk, then glue in place. Tie the end of the silver reel (rose) wire to the trunk and wind it round the sphere to secure. Cut the blue pine (spruce) into 15cm/6in lengths and trim the foliage from the stems. Push the bare stems into the sphere. Fill small gaps with moss.

3 Thread a stub wire through the bottom "leaves" of each fir cone, leaving a long length of wire. Add them to the tree, standing back to check the shape.

4 Carefully drill a hole through the base of each nut, holding it in a vice. Push a stub wire through the hole so it extends equally either side, then cross the ends and twist together. Insert into the tree. (Alternatively, you can attach the nuts to the tree with a glue gun.)

6 Cover the base of the trunk and the pot with handfuls of moss. To decorate the large tree, use a bunch of garden canes cut to length and tied with a ribbon bow.

Rosehip Tree

Scarlet rosehips are the perfect decoration for this little evergreen "tree", which is very simple to make.

MATERIALS

*damp sphagnum moss
2.5cm/1in wire mesh netting
wirecutters
18cm/7in diameter flowerpot
florist's adhesive tape
secateurs (pruning shears)
clippings of glossy evergreens,
e.g. box (boxwood)
rosehips
false berries (optional)*

1 Place the moss on the wire mesh netting, turn the corners into the centre to enclose the moss and crush the wire into a ball shape. Tuck in or cut off any stray ends with wirecutters. Place the wire ball on the flowerpot and secure it with two or three short lengths of adhesive tape. Cut the evergreens to more or less equal lengths and push the stems into the wire ball.

2 Continue filling in the ball with evergreens, then push in the rosehips and, if you are using them, the stems of false berries.

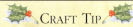

CRAFT TIP

Put this pretty rosehip tree in a porch, fireplace or a room corner where there is enough light to enhance the colour of the leaves. It makes a nice alternative to an evergreen Christmas tree.

Candy Centrepiece

Silvery lavender makes an unusual tree, decorated with ribbon and shiny wrapped candies.

MATERIALS

plastic florist's spike
23cm/9in high florist's foam cone
florist's adhesive clay
pedestal cake stand
scissors
lavender
wirecutters
medium stub wires
shiny wrapped candies
1.5cm/½in wide ribbon

3 Cut the stub wires in half, push them through the candy paper wrappings (not through the candy itself) and twist the ends. Insert the candies at intervals all around the cone.

4 Twist a wire around the centre of two lengths of ribbon and press the ends into the top of the cone.

1 Insert the spike into the base of the foam cone. Press a piece of florist's clay on to the base of the spike and press it on to the cake stand. The surface should be absolutely dry.

2 Cut the lavender stems to graduated lengths, the longest extending beyond the rim of the stand and the others successively shorter, to achieve a conical shape. Position the stems around the foam cone.

CRAFT TIP

To further enhance the glamourous effect of this irresistible centrepiece, you could first spray-paint the branches gold or silver. The finished decoration will look its best under a spotlight or in the middle of a table.

Mini Christmas Tree

Mixed evergreens, traditionally decorated with baubles and ribbon,

make the most of clippings from a garden.

MATERIALS

damp sphagnum moss
2.5cm/1in wire mesh netting
wirecutters
florist's adhesive clay
pinholder
18cm/7in diameter round basket
stout twig
medium stub wires
secateurs (pruning shears)
evergreens, such as cypress, sage and box (boxwood)
dried hydrangeas
gold baubles
7.5cm/3in wide gold ribbon

1 Place the moss on the wire mesh netting and shape it into a cone. Trim off the excess netting at the top and tuck in any stray ends of wire. Press a large piece of adhesive clay on to the base of the pinholder, then press the pinholder on to the base of the basket. Push the twig on to the pinholder. Secure it using two stub wires attached to the sides of the basket, wrapping the wires around the twig. Place the cone on the twig and secure it by taking wires from side to side and around the twig.

2 Arrange the evergreens to form a conical shape. Decorate the tree with dried hydrangeas and gold baubles. Glue a gold bow at the front of the basket to finish.

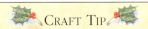 CRAFT TIP

*S*ave all the evergreen cuttings from your garden and choose only the best ones to make this decorated tree. The grey-green colours of the tree contrast beautifully with the gold baubles.

CHRISTMAS SWAG

Honesty, poppies and Chinese lanterns (winter cherry) make a lovely

indoor decoration, studded with metallic birds.

MATERIALS

secateurs (pruning shears)
dried honesty, poppy and Chinese lantern
(winter cherry) seedheads
dried sage
silver reel (rose) wire
ready-made raffia plait (braid), available
from florist's suppliers
hot glue gun or medium stub wires
bird tree decorations, on wires

1 Cut all the dried materials into stems of equal length. Using silver reel (rose) wire, bind them into mixed bunches. Attach the bunches to the raffia plait (braid), using a glue gun or stub wires bent into U-shaped staples, so that some face to either side.

2 Insert the wires of each bird through the plait (braid). With the birds in place, the swag is ready to hang on an interior door. The dried materials are too fragile to brave harsh winter climates.

TABLE CENTREPIECE

Arrange fresh flowers, fruits and evergreens in a rich display that would steal the limelight

on a sideboard or buffet table.

MATERIALS

scissors
florist's adhesive clay
2 plastic florist's spikes
large, flat plate
2 blocks of florist's foam, soaked in water
florist's scissors
evergreens, such as mahonia, yew,
cypress, ivy and eucalyptus
pineapple
carnations
roses
spray chrysanthemums
iris berries
clear quick-setting glue or hot glue gun
lychees
assorted nuts
satsumas
gold spray paint

2 Lean the pineapple against the central foam block. Secure with a stub wire wrapped around the stem and with the ends pushed into the foam. Position the carnations and roses behind the pineapple, creating a fan shape.

4 Using clear, quick-setting glue or a hot glue gun, glue several lychees into a cluster. Push a stub wire through a gap between the lychee cases, twist the ends and push them into the foam. Form a nut cluster in a similar way and position it on the other side of the design. Thread a stub wire through the back of a satsuma, twist the ends and push into the foam above the lychees.

5 Complete the design with sprays of ivy spattered with gold spray paint. Turn the arrangement around and complete the back of the centrepiece with sprays of ivy and cypress.

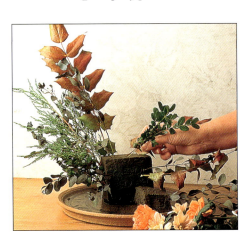

1 Cut two strips of adhesive clay and press one on to the underside of each plastic spike. Making sure that the plate is absolutely dry, press the spikes on to it, one just behind the centre and one in front to the right. Push the blocks of foam on to the spikes. Outline the arrangement with evergreens, the tallest ones at the centre back and low on the right.

3 Position short stems of ivy and spray chrysanthemums as "fillers" between the main flowers. Arrange the iris berries on stems of graduating height to distribute their contrasting texture throughout the design.

CRAFT TIP

Make your selection of fruits, flowers and nuts with an eye to colour, scale and texture. Your arrangement will look most effective when contrasting shapes are positioned next to each other.

CHRISTMAS CANDLE POT

A candle pot makes a wonderful, rich centrepiece for the table.

MATERIALS

knife
1 block florist's foam
terracotta pot
candle
medium stub wires
florist's tape (stem-
wrap tape)
hay
blue pine (spruce)
secateurs (pruning shears)
reindeer moss
mossing (floral) pins
small dried red roses
fir cones
dried mushrooms and dried kutchi fruit
(alternatively, use cinnamon sticks and
slices of dried orange)

2 Add slightly shorter pieces of pine to make a layer above the first. Continue to build up a pyramid shape, keeping the pine well away from the candle. Use stub wires to strengthen or lengthen the shorter pieces.

3 Fill any large spaces in the display with moss, attaching it with mossing (floral) pins. Put plenty of moss around the base of the candle to hide the tape.

1 Cut the foam to fit the pot, then secure the candle on top, using stub wires and florist's tape (stem-wrap tape). Fix the foam into the pot, packing any spaces with hay. Group the blue pine (spruce) into pieces of various sizes. Trim the needles from the ends of the stems. Push the largest pieces into the base of the foam, so they lean down slightly.

4 Wire the roses into bunches, using stub wires, then wire the fir cones and other material. Add to spaces in the display to create a balanced arrangement.

Advent Candle Centrepiece

Traditionally, the four Advent candles are burned for an hour on each Sunday

leading up to Christmas. On the first Sunday, one candle is burned for an hour;

on the second Sunday it is burned alongside the second candle, and so on.

MATERIALS

florist's foam brick
plate
church or beeswax candles
bunch of tree ivy
secateurs (pruning shears)
picture framer's gilt wax
fine wire
wirecutters
10 Chinese lanterns (winter cherries)

1 Soak the florist's foam brick in water and set it on a plate. Carefully push the candles into the foam.

2 Cut the tree ivy stems to size and push them into the florist's foam. Gild the berries with picture framer's gilt wax.

3 Pass a wire through the base of each Chinese lantern (winter cherry), then twist the ends together. Push the twisted wire ends into the florist's foam base.

Evergreen Winter Candles

Candlelight in a window gives pleasure to those inside the room and to others who pass by outside.

MATERIALS

*knife
florist's adhesive clay
florist's foam holders
florist's foam,
soaked in water
tall green and white candles
wirecutters
medium stub wires
lichen
miniature evergreen tree, in
pot (optional)
selection of mixed evergreens
fir cones
fallen leaves, sprayed gold*

2 Cut the stub wires in half and bend each one in half to make U-shaped staples. Fix clumps of lichen to the foam, to conceal the fixings. Add the miniature evergreen tree in its pot, if using.

3 Arrange the evergreens in a dense mass of varying greens until all the foam is covered. Twist stub wires around the fir cones and push them into the foam at intervals throughout the design. Add the gilded leaves.

1 Cut strips of adhesive clay and press them to the undersides of the florist's foam holders. Press the soaked foam into the holders. Press the candles into the foam.

Mantelpiece Swag

This grand swag is very simply created using string and sprigs of fresh,

supple blue pine (spruce) as a base.

MATERIALS

string
silver reel (rose) wire
scissors
secateurs (pruning shears)
blue pine (spruce)
wirecutters
medium stub wires
freeze-dried artichokes
dried pomegranates
fir cones
dried red chillies
thick rope or wide ribbon

1 Make a loop of string and attach the silver reel (rose) wire to its base, twisting it around several times to secure. Measure the string to the desired length of the swag and cut. Cut sprigs of blue pine (spruce) of roughly equal length.

2 Place a sprig of blue pine over the loop, then secure with wire as tightly as possible. Continue to add a few sprigs at a time along the string.

3 Alternate sides and rotate the swag to achieve a fully rounded effect. The string should be wound into the centre of the swag to act as a core and to ensure flexibility. When you reach the end, make another loop, tie with the wire and cut.

4 Wire the artichokes and pomegranates individually. Insert them into the body of the swag in clusters of three, starting with the artichokes. Space each group evenly along the whole length of the mantelpiece swag.

5 Push the wires firmly through the body of the swag at a diagonal, then wind the ends tightly around one another to secure. Place groups of pomegranates at regular intervals between the artichoke clusters.

6 Wire the fir cones between the natural "teeth" of the cone, as close to the base as possible. Add the fir cones in groups of three at regular intervals.

7 To prepare the chillies, take three at a time and wire the stalks together. Add to the swag in large clusters between the other main groups of materials.

8 Feed rope or ribbon between the various groups. Secure it to the swag at strategic points with U-shaped pins made of short lengths of bent stub wire. Do not pull the rope or ribbon too tightly.

MANTELPIECE DECORATION

Place this elegant arrangement in front of a mirror

to make it doubly effective.

MATERIALS

polystyrene (plastic foam) balls
double-sided adhesive tape
scissors
reindeer moss
ivory candles of various sizes and heights
foil dishes
plastic adhesive
silver reel (rose) wire
ivy

3 Arrange the candles on foil dishes, then secure them in place with pieces of plastic adhesive.

1 Completely cover the polystyrene balls with double-sided adhesive tape.

4 Wire together small bunches of ivy, then attach them to longer main stems to make lush garlands. Arrange the candles on the mantelpiece and drape the ivy garlands in front. Place the moss balls around the candles.

CRAFT TIP

Never leave burning candles unattended and do not allow them to burn down to within 5cm/2in of foliage or other decorative material.

2 Press the reindeer moss gently on to the balls to cover the polystyrene. Leave to dry.

Christmas Crafts to Make and Sew

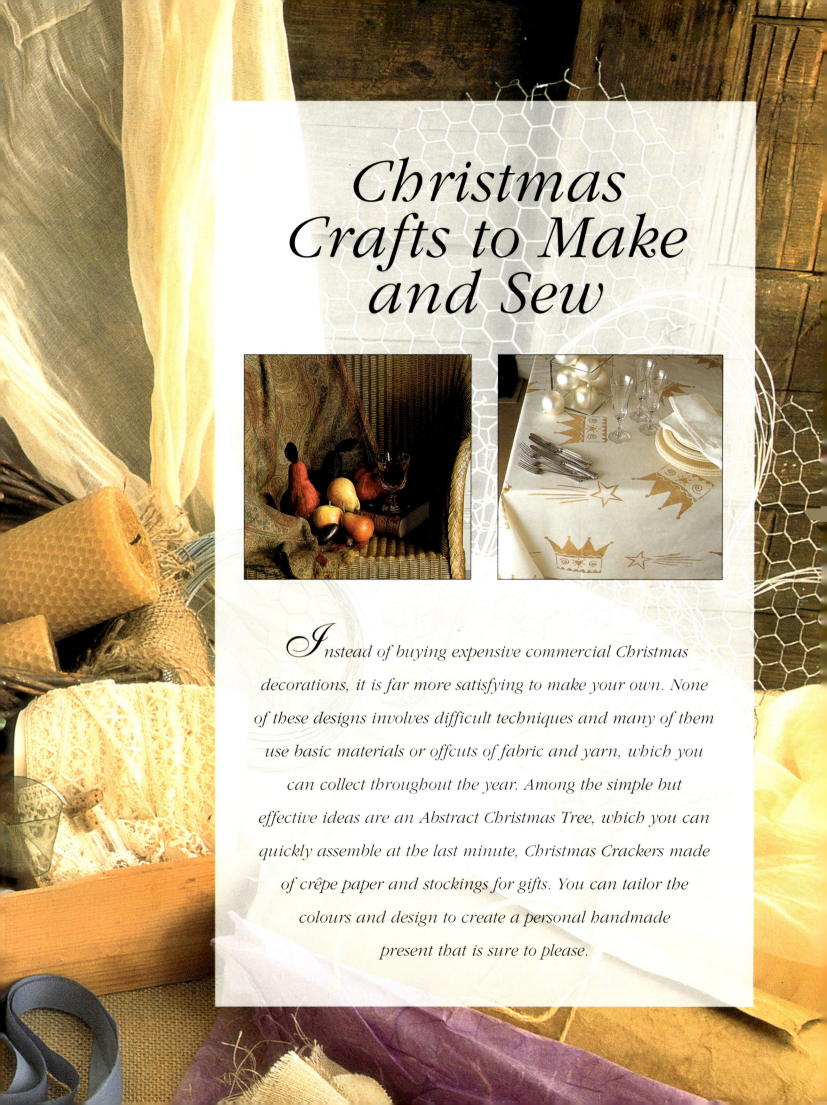

*I*nstead of buying expensive commercial Christmas decorations, it is far more satisfying to make your own. None of these designs involves difficult techniques and many of them use basic materials or offcuts of fabric and yarn, which you can collect throughout the year. Among the simple but effective ideas are an Abstract Christmas Tree, which you can quickly assemble at the last minute, Christmas Crackers made of crêpe paper and stockings for gifts. You can tailor the colours and design to create a personal handmade present that is sure to please.

Appliqué Christmas Tree

This charmingly simple little picture can be framed or mounted as a seasonal greeting for a special person.

MATERIALS

*scraps of homespun fabrics in greens, red
and orange
scissors
matching sewing threads
needle
coarse off-white cotton
dressmaker's pins
stranded embroidery thread (floss)
gold embroidery thread (floss)
embroidery needle*

1 Cut out the pieces for a simple tree shape from three different shades and textures of green fabric. Cut out a red rectangle for the background and an orange tree trunk. Join the three sections of the tree with running stitches, using matching sewing thread.

2 Pin all the pieces to a piece of off-white cotton large enough to fill the picture frame or mount.

3 Using matching threads, sew the pieces together invisibly in slip-stitch, tucking the edges under with your needle as you sew. Aim for a slightly uneven, naïve appearance. Add gold stars and coloured stitch details using three strands of embroidery thread (floss). Press the appliqué picture gently before framing or mounting.

CRAFT TIP

For the best effect, use homespun fabrics in contrasting textures and colours, with simple, childlike stitches.

HEAVENLY GOLD STAR

Collect as many different kinds of gold paper as you can find to give subtle variations of texture.

MATERIALS

assorted gold papers – candy wrappers,
metallic crêpe paper, gift-wrap, etc
PVA (white) glue
artist's paintbrush
polystyrene (plastic foam) star
fine wire
scissors
masking tape
gold glitter paint

3 Make a loop of wire and stick the ends into the back of the star for hanging. Secure with masking tape. Cover the back with gold paper in the same way as the front.

4 Leave the glue until it is completely dry, then cover the whole star with a coat of gold glitter paint.

1 Tear the various gold papers into odd shapes of slightly different sizes.

2 Dilute PVA (white) glue with a little water. Paint it on to the back of a piece of gold paper and stick on to the polystyrene (plastic foam) star. Paint more glue over the piece to secure it. Work all over the front of the star, using different papers to vary the texture and colour.

ABSTRACT CHRISTMAS TREE

This stylish white-and-gold tree makes a lovely modern alternative to traditional decorations.

It looks best as part of a cool, monochrome arrangement in white or gold.

MATERIALS

hot glue gun
coarse sisal (parcel) string
large polystyrene (plastic foam) cone
scissors
small polystyrene (plastic foam) star
white emulsion (latex) paint
artist's paintbrush
gold paint

 CRAFT TIP

When winding the coarse sisal (parcel) string on to the cone, make sure the ends of the string are evenly spaced around the base so that the tree stands upright.

2 Wind a short length of string in a coil and glue it to the top of the cone. This coil will act as a base for the star to sit on.

4 Paint the cone and star with several coats of white emulsion (latex) paint, covering the string and filling in any dents in the polystyrene (plastic foam).

1 Using a hot glue gun, attach the end of the string to the base of the cone. Wind the string up the cone towards the point, then down to the base again, gluing it as you work and securing it when it crosses. Each time you reach the base, cut the string and start again from another point so that the cone is evenly covered.

3 Wind and glue string around the star in the same way. Hide the raw ends under the string. Glue the star to the top of the cone.

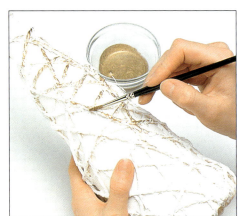

5 Finish by brushing roughly over the string with gold paint.

Santa's Toy Sack

Leave this lovely sack by the fireplace on Christmas Eve. Alternatively, it would be

a wonderful way to deliver gifts when you visit friends.

MATERIALS

tape measure
scissors
1.6 x 1.1m/63 x 43in hessian (burlap), washed
dressmaker's pins
sewing machine
selection of contrasting satin ribbons, 3.5–4.5cm/1¼–1¾in wide
bodkin or safety pin
matching sewing threads
needle

1 Trim the hessian (burlap) so that it measures 1 x 1.5m/39 x 59in. Fold it in half, right sides together, bringing the shorter sides together. Pin across the bottom and up the side, making a seam allowance of approximately 4cm/1½in.

2 Machine stitch the bottom and one side of the sack.

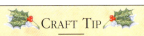

CRAFT TIP

Hessian (burlap) is not pre-shrunk, so wash the fabric before you begin to make the sack. Use your machine's hottest setting, then press with a steam iron or damp cloth to remove all the creases.

3 Still working on the wrong side, turn down the top edge by approximately 7cm/3in. Pin, then cover the raw edge with a length of satin ribbon. Fold under the raw ends of the ribbon to leave an opening. Machine stitch close to the top and bottom edges of the ribbon.

4 Using a bodkin or safety pin, thread a length of contrasting ribbon through the channel you have created. It should be long enough to make a generous bow when the top of the sack is gathered up. Turn the sack right side out.

5 Using a double thread, stitch along one edge of a length of ribbon in running stitch. Draw the ribbon up into gathers. Cut to length, allowing for joining the ends, flatten out and measure how much you need to make a rosette. Cut all the ribbons to this length. Gather each ribbon and secure tightly, then join the raw edges invisibly from the wrong side.

6 Make enough rosettes in assorted colours to make a pleasing arrangement on the front of the sack. Stitch on the rosettes by hand, using matching thread.

Velvet Stocking

This grown-up stocking is just asking to be filled with exquisite treats and presents.

MATERIALS

pencil
paper for templates
gold satin fabric
dressmaker's pins
tailor's chalk
scissors
dressweight velvet in three
toning colours
sewing machine
matching sewing thread
decorative braid
sequin ribbon
sewing needle
gold buttons

1 Copy the template for the cuff from the back of the book and enlarge to the size required. Place the template against a folded edge of gold satin. Pin, then draw around the pattern piece with tailor's chalk. Cut out two cuffs, adding a narrow seam allowance.

CRAFT TIP

This exquisite stocking looks best in rich, dark colours. Use a range of light-weight, textured and two-toned velvet colours for a Christmassy feel. The braid and sequins add an eye-catching finishing touch.

2 Make a template for the stocking in the same way and divide into three sections. Place the template for each section on a double thickness of each colour of velvet. Pin and draw around each piece with tailor's chalk. Cut out, leaving a narrow seam and pin together.

3 When the three sections of velvet and the gold cuff for each side have been pinned together, machine stitch each seam and tidy any loose ends of thread.

4 On the right side of each piece, pin a strip of decorative braid and a strip of sequin ribbon. Sew these on invisibly by hand.

5 Right sides together, machine stitch the two sides of the stocking and the cuff together. Turn through, then fold down the gold satin inside to form a deep cuff. Turn in the raw edge of the cuff and stitch down to neaten, catching it to the seams of the velvet stocking.

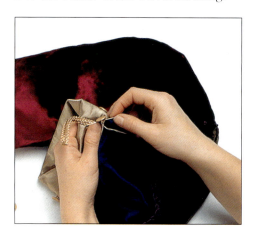

6 Trim the satin cuff with a few gold buttons. To finish, attach a loop of gold braid for hanging.

Angel Stocking

Different shades of denim work well together to make an unusual Christmas stocking.

MATERIALS

pencil
tracing paper
paper for templates
scissors
iron-on fusible
bonding web
scraps of denim,
in different shades
dressmaker's pencil or
fading fabric marker
embroidery needle
embroidery threads (floss)
buttons
dressmaker's pins
ribbon
sewing machine
matching sewing threads
pinking shears
gingham fabric

1 Trace the angel shape at the back of the book and transfer on to paper to make templates. Iron fusible bonding web on to the back of scraps of denim. Draw around the templates on to the bonding web with a dressmaker's pencil or fabric marker. Cut out the shapes.

2 Draw a large stocking shape on paper and cut out to make a template. Draw around the template on to two pieces of denim and cut out. Remove the backing paper from the bonding web. Position the appliqué shapes on the right side of one stocking piece and iron in place.

3 Decorate the angel with different embroidery stitches. Stitch features on to the face and the hair.

4 Sew buttons around the angel and scatter over the rest of the stocking.

5 Right sides facing, pin the two stocking pieces together, leaving the top edge open. Cut a 12cm/4½in length of ribbon, fold in half and trap between the two stocking pieces on one side, approximately 6cm/2½in below the top. Machine stitch the pieces, leaving a 1cm/½in seam. Neaten the raw edges with pinking shears.

6 For the lining, use pinking shears to cut two stocking shapes from gingham fabric. Right sides facing, pin them together, leaving the top edge open. Stitch, leaving a 1cm/½in seam and a 15cm/6in gap along one side.

7 Place the denim stocking inside the lining stocking, matching the top raw edges. Pin the denim and lining together around the top opening. Stitch, leaving a 1cm/½in seam.

8 Push the denim stocking through the gap in the lining, then push the lining inside the denim stocking. Slip-stitch the gap. Stitch a line of running stitch around the top edge of the stocking.

CHRISTMAS CRACKERS

Making your own Christmas crackers is very rewarding, and you can collect small gifts to put in them.

MATERIALS

double-sided crêpe paper
craft knife
metal ruler
cutting mat
thin card (cardboard) in
white and black
double-sided adhesive tape
gold crêpe paper
gold paper-backed foil
corrugated card (cardboard)
fine gold cord
cracker snaps
paper hats, jokes and
small gifts
narrow black ribbon

1 For each cracker, cut two rectangles of crêpe paper 25 x 20cm/10 x 8in, using a craft knife and cutting mat. Join, overlapping the ends, to make a rectangle 45 x 20cm/18 x 8in.

2 Cut three pieces of thin white card (cardboard) 22 x 10cm/9 x 4in. Roll each into a cylinder, overlapping the short ends by 3.5cm/1⅜in. Lay strips of double-sided adhesive tape across the crêpe paper with which to attach the card cylinders: one in the centre and the other two about 4cm/1½in from each end of the crêpe rectangle. Roll up and secure the edge with double-sided tape.

3 Decorate the cracker with strips of gold paper. To make the gold corrugated paper, lay a strip of paper-backed foil over a piece of corrugated card (cardboard) and ease the foil into the ridges with your thumb. Cut a simple star shape out of thin black card (cardboard), wrap some fine gold cord around it and stick it on top of the gold decoration.

4 Insert a cracker snap and place a paper hat, joke and gift in the central section of the cracker.

5 Tie up the ends of the cracker with narrow black ribbon, easing the crêpe paper gently so that you can tie the knots very tightly. Tie each ribbon into a large, neat bow.

6 Complete the cracker by folding the edges of the crêpe paper neatly over the ends of the cardboard cylinders.

GOLD CROWN TABLECLOTH

Set the festive tone with this lovely white-and-gold tablecloth, decorated with stencilled motifs.

MATERIALS

135cm/54in square of white cotton fabric
dressmaker's pins
pencil
tracing paper
stencil card (cardboard)
craft knife
cutting mat
masking tape
stencil brush
gold stencil paint
fine artist's paintbrush
sewing machine
white sewing thread

1 Iron the fabric to remove creases, then fold in quarters and press the folds. Fold each quarter to find the centre point, press and mark with pins. Trace the crown and shooting star templates from the back of the book, transfer on to stencil card (cardboard) and cut out with a craft knife. Stencil crowns in the corners of the tablecloth, then the edges and centre.

2 Taking care not to overload your brush, stencil shooting stars between the crowns, all pointing in the same direction around the edge of the cloth.

3 Complete the stars by touching up the gaps left by the stencil with a fine paintbrush and gold stencil paint.

4 Press on the wrong side of the fabric to fix the paint. Hem the fabric all around the edge on a sewing machine, using matching thread.

FESTIVE WINE GLASSES

Transform plain wine glasses with stained-glass colours, to give the effect of a medieval feast.

MATERIALS

*plain wine glasses
white spirit (paint
thinner)
gold glass (relief) outliner
oil-based glass paints
fine artist's paintbrush
old glass or jar*

3 Check the colour and get the feel of the glass paint by practising on an old glass or jar first. Use a fine paintbrush to colour in your design, and be careful not to get paint on the gold outliner. Try to finish each colour before changing to the next one. Clean the brush with white spirit between each colour.

1 Wash the glasses with detergent, then wipe over with white spirit (paint thinner) to remove all traces of grease.

2 Pipe your design directly on to the glass with gold glass (relief) outliner. (It's best to avoid the rim of the glass as the outliner will feel bumpy against the drinker's lips.) Leave to dry thoroughly for at least 24 hours.

Christmas Tree Decorations

*D*ecorations for the Christmas tree can be made from an enormous array of different materials, including reflective papers, gingerbread, papier-mâché and modelling clay. You can make tassels or delicate insects out of embroidery threads (floss), or gild fruit, eggs or shells with gold or silver spray paint, gilt cream or metal leaf. Salt dough shapes and tin decorations have great folk art appeal, and the Heraldic Decorations and the Wire Angel have the same simple charm. For a traditional Victorian tree, choose spangly decorations such as the Sequinned Baubles, or you can experiment with the spectacular Exotic Ornaments.

FRUIT AND SPICE ORNAMENTS

Natural materials add a splash of colour and a delightful fresh scent to the Christmas tree.

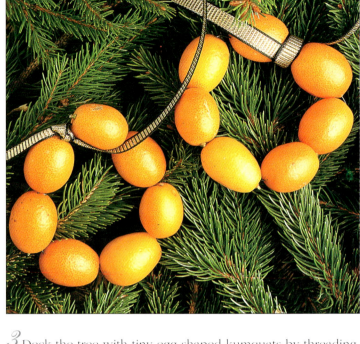

1 Tie decorative bundles of cinnamon sticks together with ribbon for a spicy decoration, then glue red cranberries to the ribbon. Thread garlands of cranberries on to sewing thread and drape over the tree.

3 Deck the tree with tiny egg-shaped kumquats by threading them on to medium stub wires. Loop the kumquat circlets over the tree branches, or tie them with ribbon. You could also use satsumas, tangerines or clementines.

2 Thick dried orange rings look good enough to eat. Cut 5mm/¼in slices from a large orange, place on a rack and dry in an oven at a low temperature for about 1 hour. Push a knife through each slice just below the peel and thread with ribbon.

4 These unusual ornaments are made by gluing a small white cake candle to the base of a white curtain ring. Cut a piece of gold sequin trim to fit the curtain ring and glue it on the back of the ring. Spray a star anise gold and glue to the front.

SPICY POMANDERS

Pomanders have been a favourite Christmas decoration since Elizabethan times.

MATERIALS

navel or thin-skinned oranges
cloves
masking tape
large paperclips
narrow ribbon

CRAFT TIP

There are many classic pomander designs based on geometric patterns such as circles, squares and stars. The pomanders shown here were slashed vertically with a knife in a design reminiscent of a Renaissance doublet.

1 Stud the oranges with cloves. For a traditional design, wrap masking tape around the fruit in a criss-cross fashion to divide it into four equal sections, then outline the tape with cloves.

2 Push the loop of a large paperclip deep into the top of each fruit to make a loop. Keep the fruit in a warm cupboard for 1–2 weeks, then thread ribbon through the loops for hanging.

GILDED GLASS

Transform plain Christmas tree balls into unique ornaments – simple designs such as

circles, triangles and stars work best.

MATERIALS

plain glass balls
detergent
white spirit (paint thinner)
gold glass (relief) outliner
kitchen paper towels
jam jars
wire-edged or other wide ribbon
scissors

1 Clean the balls carefully with detergent and white spirit. Working on one side, squeeze outliner on to the glass in a simple design. Wipe off any mistakes with kitchen paper towels before they dry.

2 Rest each ball in an empty jam jar and leave for 24 hours to dry thoroughly. Decorate the other side and leave to dry again. Thread ribbon through the hanging loop and tie in a bow.

 CRAFT TIP

Simple, bold shapes look best on small balls. Take your inspiration from stained glass windows in churches, mixing geometric shapes with elegant curves or curlicues.

INDIAN-STYLE DECORATIONS

These unusual salt dough ornaments evoke the vivid colours of an Indian festival.

MATERIALS

*225g/8oz/2 cups plain flour,
plus extra for dusting
115g/4oz/1 cup salt
250ml/8fl oz/1 cup tepid water
rolling pin
baking paper (parchment)
scissors
sharp knife
cocktail stick (toothpick) or drinking straw
baking sheet
medium and fine artist's paintbrushes
acrylic gesso
paints in bright colours
strong glue
selection of beads and sequins
matt acrylic varnish and brush
narrow ribbon*

3 Make smaller templates of the relief designs, cut out in dough and stick them to the ornaments. Place on a baking sheet and bake at 120°C/250°F/ Gas ½ for 5 hours. Cool.

4 Prime with acrylic gesso. Leave to dry, then paint in bright colours. Glue on beads and sequins. Coat with acrylic varnish when dry. Thread ribbon through the holes for hanging.

1 Mix the flour, salt and half the water, then gradually add more water. Knead for 10 minutes. Roll out the dough on baking paper (parchment). Enlarge the templates from the back of the book on a photocopier. Carefully cut out the templates, place on the dough and cut out the designs with a sharp knife.

2 Dust the dough with flour. Make the patterns and details in the dough using a cocktail stick (toothpick) or drinking straw. Make a hole in the top of each shape for hanging. Moisten the ornaments with a little water.

Sequinned Stars

Shimmering sequins and tiny beads make these lovely decorations really shine.

MATERIALS

polystyrene (plastic foam) star with
hanging loop
gold spray paint
small piece of modelling clay
brown paper
multicoloured glass seed beads
multicoloured sequins
seed pearl beads
special design sequins
1.5cm/⅝in brass-beaded pins
thin gold braid
scissors

1 Spray the polystyrene (plastic foam) star with gold paint, anchoring it with a piece of modelling clay to some brown paper to stop it moving. Allow to dry.

2 While the star is drying, sort all the beads, sequins and pins into separate containers to make it easier to choose colours and shapes as you work.

3 Thread a glass bead on to a pin, followed by a multicoloured sequin. Push it gently into the star. Repeat to complete the design, covering the whole star. Pin a seed pearl bead and special design sequin in the centre of each side of the star.

4 For an alternative design, decorate the edges of the star with lines of sequins in contrasting colours. Pick out the ridges of the star in the same way, leaving the inner sections gold. Thread gold braid through the loops of the stars for hanging.

GLITTERING FIR CONES

The intricate shape of fir cones looks wonderful highlighted with gold and silver paint and glitter.

MATERIALS

fir cones
red oxide spray primer
spray paints in gold and silver
hot glue gun or all-purpose glue and
an old, fine paintbrush
assorted glitters
saucer
ribbon

1 To provide a good base colour for the spray paint, spray the fir cones with red oxide primer. Leave to dry for 1–2 hours, then check that all the recesses and details are well covered.

3 Heat a glue gun and apply a little glue to the tips of each cone, taking care not to apply too much. Alternatively, apply small dabs of glue on to the cone tips with an old, fine paintbrush.

4 Working quickly, sprinkle glitter on to the fir cones so that it sticks to the glued tips. Use a saucer to catch the excess glitter. When dry, glue a length of ribbon to the base of each cone.

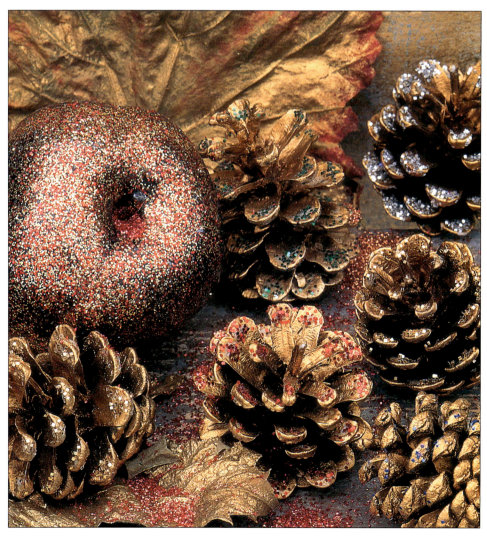

2 Spray each cone several times with gold or silver spray. Hold the can 25–30cm/10–12in away from the cone as you spray and take care to cover the whole cone. Set the cones aside until they are completely dry.

Heraldic Decorations

These stylish salt dough decorations look good enough to eat, but are purely ornamental.

MATERIALS

225g/8oz/2 cups plain flour
115g/4oz/1 cup salt
250ml/8fl oz/1 cup tepid water
rolling pin
baking paper (parchment)
pencil
tracing paper
scissors
small, sharp knife
boiled sweets (hard candies)
cocktail stick (toothpick)
artist's paintbrushes
acrylic gesso
gold craft paint
water-based satin varnish
jewels or sequins (optional)
strong glue (optional)
fine gold cord

1 Mix the flour, salt and water to a firm dough. Knead for 10 minutes. Roll the dough out flat on baking paper (parchment) to a thickness of 5mm/¼in. Trace the templates at the back of the book and cut out of the dough. Dust with flour and place a sweet in the centre. Cut around each sweet, adding a 2mm/⅛in margin.

2 Make a hole in the top of each shape with a cocktail stick (toothpick). Transfer the ornaments, without the sweets, on the paper to a baking sheet and bake at 120°C/250°F/Gas ½ for 9 hours. Place a boiled sweet in each hole and return to the oven for 30 minutes. Remove from the oven and set aside to cool.

3 Paint the shapes with gesso and allow to dry. Then paint with gold paint and allow to dry overnight. Apply five coats of varnish, leaving to dry between applications. Jewels or sequins can also be added at this stage by gluing them on to the surface of the decorations. Thread gold cord through the holes for hanging.

CRAFT TIP

Jewels, sequins and colourful painted patterns can be used to enhance classic shapes such as fleurs-de-lys and stars.

PAPIER-MÂCHÉ DECORATIONS

These colourful ornaments are easy to make from scraps of newspaper.

MATERIALS

pencil
thin card (cardboard)
craft knife
cutting mat
strong clear glue and brush
small metal jewellery findings
newspaper
PVA (white) glue, diluted with water
artist's paintbrushes
white emulsion (latex) paint
pencil
poster paints
clear gloss varnish and brush
thin cord

1 Draw a heart, bell and bauble shape and transfer them to card (cardboard). Cut out, using a craft knife and cutting mat. Glue a jewellery finding on to the top of each shape, at the back. When the glue is dry, cover the card shapes with three layers of thin newspaper strips soaked in diluted PVA (white) glue. Dry overnight, then prime with a coat of white emulsion (latex) paint.

2 When dry, draw a design on each shape in pencil, then paint with poster paints. Seal with a coat of varnish. Thread cord through the findings and tie the ends in a knot for hanging.

Sequinned Baubles

Sequins make wonderful Christmas decorations, twinkling and sparkling as they catch the light.

MATERIALS

marker pen
2 compressed cotton spheres,
6cm/2½in diameter
5mm/¼in diameter round concave
sequins in various colours,
including metallic
lill pins
beading needle
beading thread
small bronze-coloured glass beads
fruited metal beads
dressmaker's pins
silver pointed oval sequins
ribbon (optional)

2 Outline the sections with round concave sequins, using a variety of different colours. Use lill pins to attach the sequins to the sphere and overlap each one slightly.

5 To make the star bauble, mark several horizontal stripes. Press in a sequin at the top and bottom. Working outwards from these points, press in silver pointed sequins to form a star shape.

1 Using a marker pen, divide the surface of the first cotton sphere into quarters, as shown. Mark around the middle of the sphere to divide it into eight sections.

3 Fill in the sections, again overlapping the sequins slightly.

6 Fill in the rest of sphere with round sequins, as in steps 2 and 3. As an alternative hanging loop, attach a 10cm/4in piece of ribbon to the top, using a dressmaker's pin and metal bead as in step 4.

 CRAFT TIP

*C*ollect as many different colours and shapes of sequins as you can for making these sparkly Christmas baubles. Sequins come in all shapes and sizes, including circles, stars and flower shapes.

4 Using a beading needle and thread, make several small stitches in the top of the sphere. Thread on 8cm/3in of small bronze glass beads, then make several stitches to make a loop for hanging. Thread a metal bead on to a pin and press into the sphere to secure the loop.

WIRE ANGEL

Soft wire bends easily into loops and curls to make a beautiful adornment to hang

from the tree or from a Christmas wreath.

MATERIALS

1mm/¹⁄₂in thick silver- or gold-plated
copper wire
round-nosed pliers
parallel (channel-type) pliers
wirecutters
narrow ribbon
star-shaped bead or crystal droplet

1 Use the template at the back of the book as a guide for shaping the wire, either at the same size or enlarged.

2 Leaving 5cm/2in at the end, start bending the wire around the template, using round-nosed pliers and your fingers. Make the hair curls and the forehead up to the eye. Make the lower lid of the eye first and then the upper lid. Halfway along the upper lid, make a loop around the end of the round-nosed pliers to form the pupil. Squeeze the corner of the eye with parallel (channel-type) pliers.

3 Shape the nose and make a larger loop around the end of the round-nosed pliers for the nostril. Shape the mouth, closing the lips with parallel pliers, then shape the chin.

4 Loop the wire around the bottom of the hair to make the cheek. This loop will help to keep the structure flat and more manageable.

5 Follow the template along the arm. Make loops with the round-nosed pliers for the fingers, then shape the bottom line of the arm.

6 Make the shoulder by carefully looping the wire around the point where the arm joins the neck.

7 At the waist, bend the wire across to form the waistband. Make a series of long horizontal loops with slightly curled ends back along the waistband. When you have made seven loops, secure with a tight twist at the bend.

8 Make a large curve for the lower part of the skirt. Shape a wavy hem around the thickest part of the round-nosed pliers. The legs interrupt the wavy hemline. Make the toes in the same way as the fingers, but they should be shorter and rounder. Shape the heels and make a small decorative loop at each ankle.

9 Complete the wavy hemline and the back of the skirt. Secure by twisting the wire tightly around the waistband.

10 Make loops along the bottom of the wing and close slightly to neaten. Form the curved top of the wing.

11 Loop the wire around the back of the shoulder and under the bottom of the wing. Finish off with a coil and cut off the wire.

12 Using the 5cm/2in of wire left at the start, bind the shoulder and wing together. Cut off the end. Thread ribbon through the loops in the waistband and hang a star-shaped bead or crystal droplet from the angel's hand.

Festive Figures

Use Christmas-themed pastry (cookie) cutters to make these clay shapes,

then embellish them with bronze powder and rhinestones.

MATERIALS

polymer clay
rolling pin
Christmas-themed pastry
(cookie) cutters
modelling tool
paintbrush
plastic straw
bronze powders in various colours
varnish and brush
rhinestones
glue
toothpick
ribbon

2 Draw on markings with a modelling tool. Make small indentations for the rhinestones with the end of a paintbrush.

5 When cool, use a paintbrush to apply a coat of varnish. This will protect the figure from scratches.

1 Roll out some clay and press out a shape using a pastry (cookie) cutter.

3 Using a plastic straw, make a hole in the centre top for hanging.

6 Glue rhinestones in the indentations, with the aid of a toothpick. Thread ribbon through the hole for hanging.

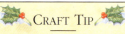 CRAFT TIP

Polymer clay is actually a plastic, but has all the advantages of clay: it can be moulded, modelled, sculpted, stretched and embossed prior to being baked. It does not require firing at high temperatures: bake it in an ordinary domestic oven at 102–135°C/215–275°F/Gas ½–1 according to the manufacturer's instructions. This transforms the clay from a malleable substance into a solid one. Once baked, the clay can be sanded, sawn, drilled and glued.

4 Brush on different-coloured bronze powders and blend together. Bake the figures in the oven, following the manufacturer's instructions.

FELT STARS

Red and green, the traditional festive colours, are mixed and matched in these two simple designs.

MATERIALS

*pencil
paper or thin card (cardboard)
scissors
tailor's chalk
red and green felt
embroidery scissors
needle
matching sewing threads
scraps of patterned fabric
ribbon*

1 Draw a star shape on to paper or thin card (cardboard) and make a template. Using tailor's chalk, draw around the template on to felt.

2 Use a pair of embroidery scissors to cut equal numbers of red and green stars from the felt.

3 Using the point of the embroidery scissors, pierce one of the red stars 5mm/¼in from the edge. Cut out a smaller star, leaving a 5mm/¼in border all around.

4 Stitch the red border to one of the green stars with small, even running stitches and matching thread.

5 Centre a small red star as cut out in step 3 on a green star. Stitch in place.

6 Place the stars from steps 4 and 5 together, sandwiching a plain red star in the middle. Stitch the three stars together at the inner points, as shown.

7 For a different decoration, take a green felt star and cut a small circle from the centre. Place on top of a red star, with a small piece of patterned fabric showing through the hole. Sew neatly around the hole in running stitch.

8 Stitch the two stars together around the edges with stab stitch.

9 Use a loop of coloured ribbon for hanging. Alternatively, wrap sewing thread around all four fingers, then stitch a loop on to a point of each star with small stitches.

RIBBONS AND BOWS

Hang these lovely, delicate decorations on the tree or on a length of gold ribbon

strung across the mantelpiece.

MATERIALS

For the Baubles
pencil
polystyrene (plastic foam) balls,
7.5 or 5cm/3 or 2in
in diameter
gold, brown and cream ribbons,
1m x 3–9mm/40in x ⅛–⅜in
dressmaker's pins
scissors
toning patterned ribbon,
2m x 3–9mm/2¼yd x ⅛–⅜in
tiny gold beads
gold-coin pendants
large, ornate gold beads

For the Fir Cone Parcels
gold, lemon or brown ribbon,
4cm/1½in wide
gold or brown ribbon, 3mm/⅛in wide
fir cones
all-purpose glue

For the Golden Tassels
scissors
cotton-pulp ball, 2.5cm/1in in diameter
gold grosgrain ribbon, 9.9m x 3mm/
11yd x ⅛in
tape measure
crewel needle
all-purpose glue

BAUBLES

1 Use a pencil to divide a polystyrene (plastic foam) ball into quarters vertically, then into eighths with a horizontal line around the middle. Place a length of ribbon across one section, pin at each end on the drawn lines and cut off the ribbon. Continue filling in the section, using the assorted ribbons like patchwork, overlapping the ribbon edges and laying the ribbon smoothly over the ball.

2 Fill in all the sections, completely covering the ball. Lay the patterned ribbon along the drawn lines, covering the pins and ribbon ends. Pin in position at each point where the pencil lines cross, turning the ribbon ends under to neaten. To make a loop for hanging, slip a 25cm/10in length of ribbon under one intersection. Knot the ends together.

3 Take several pins and slip a tiny gold bead followed by a gold-coin pendant on to each one. Pin them in a row around the bauble. Thread a small bead and then a large, ornate bead on to the last pin and stick it into the base to complete.

FIR CONE PARCELS

1 Make a bow with the wide ribbon. Wrap the narrow ribbon around the fir cone as if wrapping a parcel. Tie the ribbon ends together 10cm/4in above the top of the cone to make a hanging loop. Glue the bow on top of the cone.

GOLDEN TASSELS

1 Use scissors to make a hole through the centre of the cotton-pulp ball. Pull out some of the fibre to enlarge the hole to 1cm/½in diameter.

2 Cut a 25cm/10in length from the ribbon and cut the remainder into 30cm/12in lengths. Put the 25cm/10in length and one 30cm/12in length to one side and insert the remainder through the hole, a few at a time. Use the crewel needle to thread them through if necessary. Allow 12.5cm/5in of each ribbon to hang below the ball. Dab a little glue on to the ball and fold down the ribbons protruding from the top around the outside of the ball. Continue until the ball is completely covered with ribbon.

5 To suspend the tassel, double the 30cm/12in length of ribbon and thread it on to the needle. Insert the needle down through the hole in the ball. Remove the needle, knot the ends neatly together and trim. Gently pull the loop taut, hiding the knot among the ribbons. Trim the ribbon ends to an even length.

3 Thread the needle with the 25cm/10in length of ribbon. Glue one end around the ribbons close to the base of the ball. Wrap the ribbon tightly around the tassel.

4 Insert the needle behind the binding ribbon and pull tightly. Unthread the needle, allowing the ribbon end to hang down with the other ribbons. Do not trim at this stage.

Glitter Keys

Transform everyday objects into fantasy tree decorations.

MATERIALS

old keys in various shapes and sizes
PVA (white) glue
old paintbrush
sheets of scrap paper
coloured glitter
fine gold cord

1 Using an old paintbrush, cover one side of a key with a coat of undiluted PVA (white) glue.

2 Lay the key on a sheet of scrap paper and sprinkle generously with glitter. Repeat with the other keys, using a separate sheet of paper for each one. Allow to dry completely.

3 Remove the keys. Pinch the paper to make a groove for the spare glitter to run into, then pour it back into the container. Glue the remaining uncovered areas of the keys and repeat the process. Add further layers of glitter to build up quite a thick coating. Tie a loop of gold cord to each key for hanging.

CRAFT TIP

*P*VA (white) glue dries to a transparent glaze, so you can brush it on over glitter you have already applied.

Jewelled Keys

Gold paint and fake gems turn a bunch of old keys into something fit to unlock

a fairy-tale castle or treasure chest.

MATERIALS

old keys in assorted shapes and sizes
newspaper
gold spray paint
gold braid
hot glue gun
flat-backed fake gems in
assorted colours

3 Cover the ends of the gold braid by gluing fake gems over them. Arrange two or three more jewels on the key and glue them on. Allow all the finished keys to dry thoroughly before attaching them to crackers or hanging them on the Christmas tree.

1 Make sure the keys are free of rust. Working with one side at a time and over newspaper, spray each key with gold paint and allow to dry.

2 Cut the gold braid to a suitable length for hanging the key. Fold in half and attach the ends to the key with a hot glue gun.

Sumptuous Rosettes

These flower-like ornaments can be hung on the tree or used to decorate a gift for someone special.

MATERIALS

pencil
paper for template
scissors
small pieces of silk, gold lamé or
dressweight velvet
dressmaker's pins
scissors
matching sewing thread
needle
fine gold cord
hot glue gun or strong glue
ornate buttons

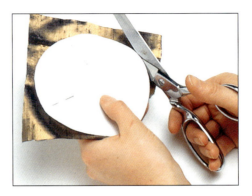

1 Draw and cut out a circular template about 12cm/4½in in diameter. Pin it to a single layer of fabric and cut out (there is no need for a seam allowance).

2 Using double thread, sew in running stitch all around the circle 5mm/¼in from the edge. Pull the thread taut to form a rosette and fasten off the ends.

3 Thread a loop of fine gold cord through the top of the rosette for hanging the decoration.

4 Using a hot glue gun, attach a button in the centre of the rosette to cover the raw edges. Alternatively, use strong glue.

EXOTIC ORNAMENTS

These sequinned and beaded balls look like priceless Fabergé treasures, yet they're simple and fun to make.

MATERIALS

scissors
paper
dressmaker's pins
gold netting
silk-covered polystyrene (plastic foam) balls
double-sided adhesive tape
gold braid
sequins in a variety of shapes and colours
small glass and pearl beads
1cm/½in long brass-headed pins
narrow ribbon

3 For an alternative design, cut lengths of gold braid and pin around the ball to make a framework for the rows of sequins.

CRAFT TIP

When you are working out your designs, use simple repeating patterns and avoid having too many colours on the same ball.

4 Attach a loop of gold thread to the ball with a brass-headed pin. Thread a bead and sequin on to a brass-headed pin and gently press into the ball. Repeat until your chosen design is complete. Thread ribbon through the loops for hanging on the Christmas tree.

1 Cut a circle of paper to completely cover the ball. Pin it to a piece of gold netting and cut out.

2 Remove the paper and attach the gold netting to the ball using tiny pieces of double-sided adhesive tape. The tape and raw edges will be hidden later by the sequins.

Natural Raffia

For a natural Christmas tree, hang up these little balls covered in creamy undyed raffia.

MATERIALS

scissors
fine copper wire
small polystyrene (plastic foam) balls
double-sided adhesive tape
natural (garden) raffia

CRAFT TIP

Use coloured raffia such as red or green for a quite different effect.

1 Cut a short piece of wire and bend it into a loop. Push the ends into a polystyrene (plastic foam) ball.

2 Cover the ball in double-sided adhesive tape, making sure there are no gaps.

3 Arrange the hank of raffia so that you can remove lengths without tangling them. Holding the first 10cm/4in of the strand at the top of the ball, wind the raffia around the ball from top to bottom.

4 When you have finished covering the ball, tie the end of the raffia to the 10cm/4in length you left free at the beginning. Using a few lengths of raffia together, form a loop for hanging and finish with a loose, floppy bow.

Twiggy Stars

These pretty stars would look equally effective hanging on the tree or in a window.

MATERIALS

willow twigs
secateurs (pruning shears)
stranded embroidery thread (floss)
scissors
check cotton fabric
natural (garden) raffia

3 Using a sharp pair of scissors, cut the check cotton fabric into strips measuring approximately 15 x 2cm/ 6 x ¾in.

4 Tie a fabric strip in a double knot over the thread securing each point of the star. Attach a loop of raffia to one point to hang the decoration.

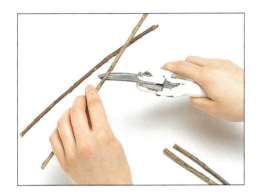

1 Cut the twigs into lengths of 15cm/ 6in using the secateurs (pruning shears). You will need five for each star.

2 Tie the first pair of twigs together near the ends with a length of embroidery thread (floss), winding it around and between to form a "V" shape. Repeat with the remaining twigs, arranging them under and over each other as shown to form a five-pointed star.

🌿 CRAFT TIP 🌿

Any straight twigs would be suitable for this project. Collect them on a winter walk.

Christmas Gift-wrapping

*M*aking your own gift-wrap and gift tags is an absorbing project for all members of the family on the evenings leading up to Christmas. Handmade gift-wrap is far more personal than any bought paper could ever be, and creating wrapping paper is fun and often quite inexpensive. Several identical sheets of gift-wrap can be produced by repeat methods such as stencilling, stamping or sponging, or you can create an impressive one-off design for a special present. Show off your creativity by placing gifts wrapped in Antique Manuscript Gift-wrap or Marbled Paper under the Christmas tree.

CHRISTMAS TREE GIFT TAGS

Mix different stencil motifs and papers to create these stylish labels.

MATERIALS

craft knife
metal ruler
cutting mat
thin card (cardboard) in
various colours
pencil
paper for template
cellulose kitchen sponge
scissors
corrugated cardboard
glue stick
stencil card (cardboard)
stencil paint in gold and black
white cartridge (heavy) paper
artist's paintbrush
watercolour inks
white oil-crayon
brown parcel wrap
(packaging paper)
hole punch
fine gold cord

2 Draw a triangular Christmas tree on to paper to make a template. Draw around this on a rectangle of kitchen sponge and cut out carefully with scissors, so that you have a positive and negative image to use as stamps. Mount each stamp on a piece of cardboard with a glue stick. Stamp both motifs in gold on to a selection of papers in different textures and colours.

5 Use a white oil-crayon to scribble spots on brown parcel wrap (packaging paper) to represent snowflakes. Tear them out individually, leaving a border of brown paper around each one.

6 Cut or tear out various motifs and arrange them on the gift tags. Attach with the glue stick. Punch a hole in the top and thread each tag with a loop of fine gold cord.

1 Using a craft knife and a metal ruler, cut out gift tags from thin card (cardboard) in various colours.

CRAFT TIP

Experiment with delicate papers such as tracing paper as well as heavier papers.

3 Draw a stylized branch pattern and transfer it to a piece of stencil card (cardboard). Cut out using a craft knife and stencil in black and gold on to a selection of papers and also on to some of the stamped tree motifs.

4 Paint plain white cartridge (heavy) paper with watercolour inks in bright colours, then cut out a simple star motif.

CRAYON GIFT-WRAP

Transform humble parcel wrap (packaging paper) into stylish and original wrapping paper.

MATERIALS

brown parcel wrap (packaging paper)
masking tape
gold paint
old plate
sponge roller
oil pastel crayons in black,
white and other colours
gold oil crayon

CRAFT TIP

The oil pastel crayons may take 24 hours, or even longer, to dry completely.

1 Secure the brown parcel wrap (packaging paper) with masking tape. Spread gold paint on an old plate. Using a sponge roller, apply the paint in wide gold lines up the sheet. Leave to dry completely.

2 Add coloured or black and white stripes to the gold, using oil pastel crayons. Leave the paper to dry thoroughly before using.

3 For an alternative look, draw vertical stripes down a piece of brown parcel wrap with a chunky gold oil crayon. Experiment with different groupings and spacings for the stripes.

ANTIQUE MANUSCRIPT GIFT-WRAP

Ancient and modern combine to make this unusual wrapping paper.

MATERIALS

piece of old manuscript
plain paper
saucers
watercolour paints in yellow
ochre and pink
artist's paintbrush
adhesive tape
scissors
ribbon

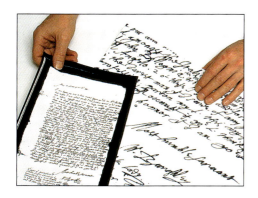

1 Photocopy a section of your chosen manuscript on to plain paper. Enlarge the copy by 200%, then make a copy of it on to larger paper.

2 Use diluted watercolour paint to tint the paper with streaks of yellow ochre and pink, giving it an antique effect. Leave to dry.

3 To wrap a round box, place it in the middle of the paper and begin pulling up the edges, sticking each section down with tape as you go. Cut a paper disc slightly smaller than the box top, and glue this on top to cover the edges.

4 Cut three equal lengths of ribbon and tie in simple knots on top of the box. Trim the ends of the ribbon to the same length.

MARBLED PAPER

Florentine marbled paper is the best in the world, so use expensive paper like this

to wrap small boxes or books.

MATERIALS

sheet of marbled paper
scissors
double-sided adhesive (cellophane) tape
narrow black satin ribbon

1 This is very precious paper, so measure accurately to avoid waste. You will need a 2.5cm/1in overlap on the top, and the side flaps should measure two-thirds the height of the box or book.

2 Tuck one edge under the other and use double-sided adhesive (cellophane) tape along the edge nearest you, peeling off the backing and pulling the paper taut before pressing one edge down on to the slight overlap.

3 Fold down the top flap, smooth around the side flaps and sharpen their edges between finger and thumbnail. Place a small piece of double-sided adhesive (cellophane) tape at the apex of the bottom flap, then fold it up and press it into the side.

4 Tie a narrow black ribbon in a simple bow for the perfect, understated way to show off this exquisite paper. Bows and decorations should be kept simple so as not to detract from the impact of the beautiful paper.

STAMPED GOLD STARS

There is something sumptuous about red tissue paper, stamped here with large gold stars.

MATERIALS

red tissue paper
scrap paper
star rubber stamp
gold ink
saucer
adhesive tape
scissors
gold ribbon

3 Trim the gift with a gold ribbon tied on top in a large bow.

4 Cut the ribbon ends at an angle for a professional finish.

1 Lay a sheet of tissue paper on scrap paper. Beginning in one corner, work diagonally across the sheet, stamping stars about 5cm/2in apart. Leave to dry.

2 Wrap the gift using a lining of one or two sheets of plain red tissue paper under the stamped sheet. Use adhesive tape to secure the ends.

CRAFT TIP

Cutting the ribbon ends at an angle looks smart and also prevents the ribbon from fraying.

WRAPPING AND TRIMMING

Not all gifts come in convenient shapes and sizes for wrapping.

WRAPPING A TEDDY BEAR

Successful gift-wrapping should both conceal and enhance your gift, adding mystery and an irresistible temptation to open up and see what is inside. An unusual shape looks great with tissue paper wrapped over cardboard.

1 Decide on a surface that is going to be the base, in this case the teddy is able to sit up. Cut out a regular shape, either square, rectangular or round, from thick cardboard. Cover with a piece of gift-wrap.

2 Place the cardboard in the middle of a large sheet of paper, or cross two lengths over for a larger gift.

3 Pull up the paper from opposite sides and bunch it up on top of the gift. Tissue paper works well for this because it creases in an attractive way. If you are using thicker paper gather and pleat it as you make the bunch.

4 Tie a ribbon or card firmly around the bunch, then arrange the paper into a balanced decorative shape. An ornament hanging down from the ribbon will help to draw attention back down to the gift.

TYING A BASIC BOW

The finishing touches to your wrapped gift are all-important. As well as using paper in a range of colours and textures, enjoy using ribbon, string and decorations to turn something ordinary into something spectacular.

1 Pass the ribbon under the gift so that you have two ends of equal length. Tie the two together on the top.

2 Knot the tied ends so that both your hands are freed for tying the bow.

3 Form two loops and tie together to make a simple bow.

4 Finish off the box by cutting the ribbon ends into swallow tails – fold the ribbon down the middle, then cut from the fold towards the open edges at an angle.

STRING AND RIBBON

A combination of coarse, thick string and smooth, silky ribbon can be used to give your gift a highly textured look. For the best effect, use a range of contrasting colours.

TAPED RIBBON

This technique produces a plain look that is very simple and yet highly elegant. Make sure that you use a good-quality ribbon; when finished, this gift needs no extra decoration.

GOLD TASSELS

Tassels like these metallic gold ones are perfect for a rich, opulent look – purple and gold make a classic combination. This style is particularly easy because you don't have to tie a bow.

COLOUR-COORDINATED

Instead of using contrasting colours, try decorating a gift with small decorations of the same colour for a really original touch – any small Christmas decorations of the same colour will look great.

1 Wrap the gift in tissue paper, then wind coarse string around the box at least four times in each direction.

1 Use a broad fancy ribbon on a plain background. Cross the ribbon over on top, then take the ends underneath.

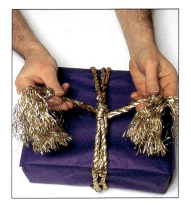

1 Wrap a gift box in several layers of deep purple tissue paper, then surround it with thick gold cord.

1 Wrap the gift in pink tissue paper and tie it with a matching pink spotted ribbon and a bow.

2 Take a short, narrow ribbon and use it to gather all the string together at the centre point. Tie a simple bow in the ribbon, then separate the strands of string out towards opposite edges of the box.

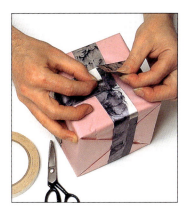

2 Instead of tying the ribbon in a bow or knot, use double-sided adhesive (cellophane) tape to join it and give a taut, flat finish without the need for additional decoration.

2 Tie a double knot and let the tasselled ends fall across the gift as a decoration. Experiment with scarves, curtain tie-backs and even pyjama cords (pajama belts).

2 Thread a Christmas pastry (cookie) cutter on to the ribbon and tie a small bow on the top to secure it. Try other small Christmas tree decorations as well.

TEMPLATES

Trace the templates directly from the page and then enlarge

or reduce to the required size with a photocopier if necessary.

Fleur-de-lis

Crown

Star

HERALDIC DECORATIONS
PAGE 66

GOLD CROWN TABLECLOTH
PAGE 56

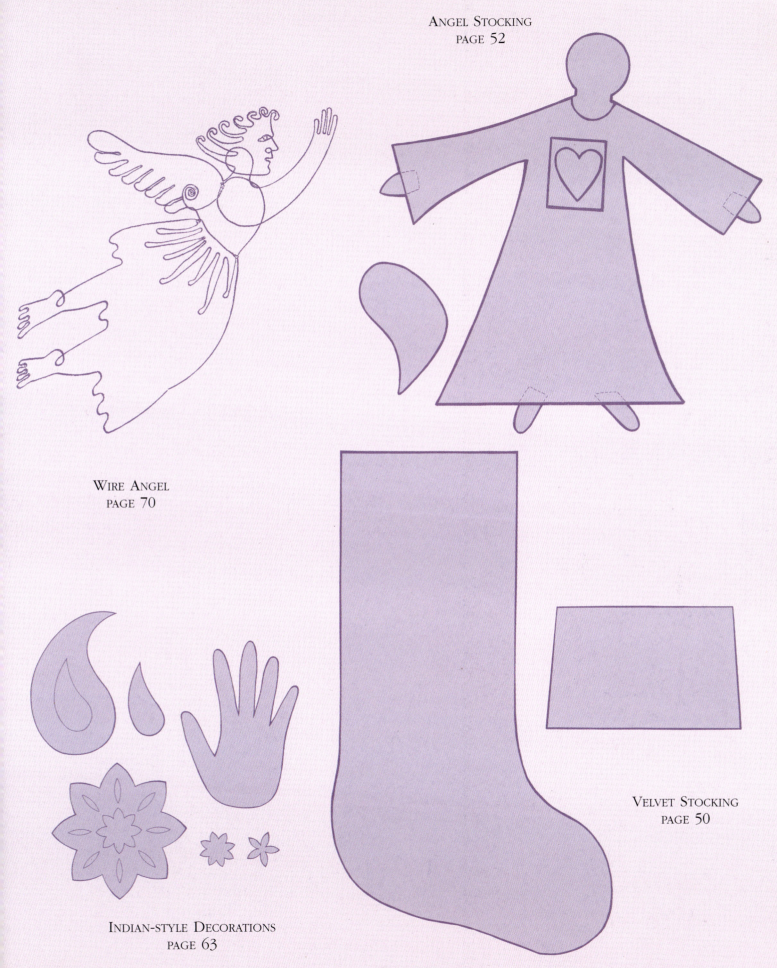

ANGEL STOCKING
PAGE 52

WIRE ANGEL
PAGE 70

VELVET STOCKING
PAGE 50

INDIAN-STYLE DECORATIONS
PAGE 63